HOW DO YOU
START
THIS
THING?

HOW DO YOU START THIS THING?

GLITCH'S 1st BOOK OF COMPUTER COMICS

Written and Illustrated by Ed Wiens

Published by GLITCH! GRAPHICS,
Edmonton, Alberta, Canada

GLITCH! GRAPHICS
Edmonton, Alberta Canada
www.glitch.ca
email: comics@glitch.ca

Printed in Canada

National Library of Canada Cataloguing in Publication Data
Wiens, Ed, 1961-
   Glitch! how do you start this thing?

   ISBN 0-9688519-0-8

   I. Title.
PN6734.G54W53 2001   741.5'971   C2001-910258-5

Acknowledgements

I would like to thank the great number of people who have made contributions to this work and to my life personally. Without their support, "GLitcH!" would only be a handful of drawings filed away in a sketchbook labeled *"Ideas That Might Work."*

I would like to thank the following people who have made personal contributions:

To begin with, I would like to thank my wife, Debbie who is my best friend and love of my life and who supports everything I do and has provided assistance, a critical eye and better judgement for GLitcH! from the beginning; and my sons Andrew and Matthew who have allowed me to experience the simple joy of being a part of their lives as they take their first steps and discover the world, one tiny stone at a time; my parents and my brother Reinhard who always noted and encouraged my love of art and drawing— a special thanks to my mother who has always helped me to pursue my interest in art. I would also like to thank all other family members and friends who have shown their interest and support for the goofy drawing that I call my work.

For their assistance and support in getting GLitcH! off the ground, I would like to thank:

Peter Collum, Business Editor of the Edmonton Journal, who took a chance and chose an absolutely unknown comic strip and gave GLitcH! its debut in a major newspaper; David Tanaka of The Computer Paper who gave GLitcH! national exposure; Brian Gerdes of TELUS Advertising Services who chose GLitcH! for the TELUS website and helped to promote it to other Yellow Pages web sites across western Canada. I would also like to thank Tom Thurston and my colleagues at the Government of Alberta, Department of Community Development, Historic Sites and Cultural Facilities Branch for their encouragement.

Amidst the work involved with the production of a new feature like GLitcH! it has been a real joy and with the association with so many fine people and their support, it has also been a privilege.

For Debbie,
Andrew and Matthew

Ed Wiens

Contents

Introduction

I work in front of a computer every day and have to admit that I've done just about everything that I could possibly do wrong on it at least once. I have a real love-hate relationship with computers. I *love* technology and opening the box of a new program is like Christmas morning for me. However, I *hate* a lot of the silly and unexpected things that computers do and the aggravating things they sometimes make *us* do. You often have to jump through digital hoops in order to operate these backlit wonder-boxes properly. Add to this the constant, mind-boggling rate of change in the technology industry and you get a pretty good reason to do a comic strip like GLitcH!

For about ten years, I had drawn cartoon illustrations occasionally for use in advertising and communications but had never considered producing my own comic strip. My last attempt at a comic strip was about a bunch of fish while I was in college in 1982, and after about five strips, I had exhausted all my ideas. It wasn't until I began GLitcH! that I thought I could do a comic strip that might actually get published.

GLitcH! was created in mid-1995 while I was doodling. The thought had run through my mind that some good advice I had once heard was that one should write (or in my case *draw*) about something that you know a lot about (which kind of explains what happened to that "fish" idea.) Because I'd been working with computers since 1986, I knew that I could draw on a lot of material from my experiences. But what kind of character could manage to do this? (*Another fish?*).

I began a new sketchbook and started filling it with sketches. After drawing my little computer character in dozens of poses, my wife looked over at it and said, "That sure is an *expressive* computer."

She was right and I was amazed to see that my computer character—which was really nothing more than a monitor for a mouth with a couple of eyeballs—could convey more emotions than my *human* cartoon characters. I added a self-animated mouse for hand gestures and a quirky, impatient and mischievous personality. After combining it with a particularly stupid human user, I discovered that I could now look at computers and technology in a unique way by both making fun of computers as well as us, the users.

It's been a lot of fun, but most cartoonists will tell you that you won't get rich doing it. They're exactly right, but I think anything at all amounts to a genuine reason for sitting in my basement drawing this crazy stuff. I hope you'll enjoy GLitcH!

Ed Wiens

GLitcH! - The Characters

In addition to the GLitcH -1000 computer, the cartoon strip is made up of the other members of the **Frazzle** family.

Norb, the father in the family, is a complete beginner at the computer. He is both confused and dazzled by technology.

Fran, the mother, doesn't share Norb's excitement with the computer and sees it mainly as a novelty or toy. She has a knack for seeing through all the computer hype.

Zack, the son, is a twelve-year-old boy who is comfortable and proficient (actually, brilliant) with computers, having grown up with computers in school.

Moddy, the daughter, is a wide-eyed six-year-old. She is neither intimidated nor excited by the computer and simply accepts it as a part of life.

Gramp, is a grumpy old grandfather who has absolutely no interest in converting to the new technological age. Gramp is not easily convinced of anything but adds some old-time common sense.

Other Characters - Other characters include the computer salesman, the indistinguishable computer techies, and a new addition to the family, a baby, also shows up occasionally.

HOW'D YOU GUYS EVER GET ALONG WITHOUT ME FOR SO LONG?

CHAPTER ONE
The Early
GLitcH!

MY NEW GLITCH-1000 COMPUTER IS HERE!

THIS SIDE UP.

GLItcH-1000

FRAGIL

"PLEASE NOTE — TO AVOID DAMAGING THE EQUIPMENT, CAUSING ELECTRIC SHOCK, HARD DRIVE OVERLOAD AND MELTDOWN, DO NOT OPEN THE BOX UNTIL READING ALL UNPACKING INSTRUCTIONS."

UP

"UNPACKING INSTRUCTIONS ARE LOCATED INSIDE THE BOX."

THIS SIDE UP

GLItcH-1000

FRAGILE

Ed Wiens © 1996 09.19.96

ARE YOU FINISHED READING ALL YOUR COMPUTER MANUALS ALREADY?

NO.

I DON'T BELIEVE IN READING MANUALS. ONE LEARNS FASTER BY JUST DOING IT.

...UH, I THINK YOU SHOULD MAKE AN EXCEPTION WHEN IT COMES TO THE INSTALLATION MANUAL!

Ed Wiens © 1996

SYSTEM ERROR... RESTART... BAD LINE CODE ... USE ANOTHER DRIVE... INSERT DISK... INITIALIZATION FAILED.

CLICK... CLICK...

THE MIND OF THE COMPUTER NOVICE IS SUCH AN EASY THING TO MESS WITH! HMM... I KNOW...

DON'T TOUCH THAT BUTTON!

... THE "AUTO-DESTRUCT" SEQUENCE HAS NOW BEEN ENGAGED... DETONATION WILL OCCUR IN TEN SECONDS... 9... 8... 7...

Ed Wiens © 1996 08.22.96

OKAY... 228 [CLICK, CLICK, CLICK] TIMES 697 [CLICK, CLICK, CLICK] EQUALS...? [ENTER] ...?

MULTIPLICATION?! I CAN DO A MILLION PROCESSES PER SECOND, AND YOU WANT ME TO ACT AS A SIMPLE CALCULATOR?

YOU'RE RIGHT. I'LL FIGURE IT OUT ON PAPER.

...AS IT SHOULD BE.

Ed Wiens © 1996

AMAZING, HOW WHEN YOU GET YOUR FIRST COMPUTER, YOU HAVE TO LEARN A WHOLE NEW LINGO!

... AND THE KEY TO LEARNING NEW TERMS IS TO USE THEM IN YOUR EVERYDAY LANGUAGE. FOR EXAMPLE...

"BUYING THIS COMPUTER TOOK A MEGABYTE OUT OF MY WALLET, AND NOW IT MEGAHERTZ!"

Ed Wiens © 1996

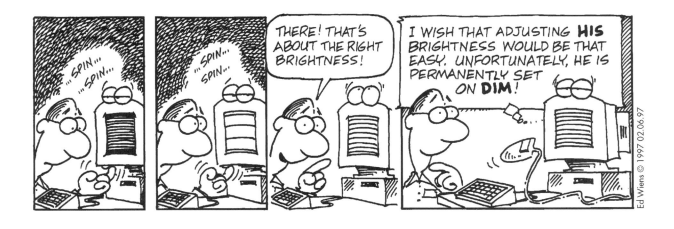

CHAPTER TWO
GLitcH!®
in the Family

"...AFTER 5 MINUTES OF NOT BEING USED, MY NEW SCREEN-SAVER SHOULD START UP ON THE COMPUTER! ...JUST WATCH!

"...TICK..." "...TICK..." "...TICK..." TICK... ...TICK..

"...TICK... BEEP!

TURN OFF THE COMPUTER OR ELSE!

... ONCE AGAIN, YOU HAVE DAZZLED ME WITH YOUR MASTERY OF TECHNOLOGY!

Ed Wiens © 1996

THE PRINTER ISN'T WORKING AGAIN. MUST BE ANOTHER COMPUTER MALFUNCTION.

MODDY, GO GET DADDY'S TOOLBOX, I'M GOING TO SHOW YOU HOW TO OPEN THE CPU AND GIVE IT A GOOD OILING!

...PRINT, PRINT, PRINT, PRINT..., PRINT, PRINT, ...PRINT, PRINT, PRINT

WHRRR

IT'S FUNNY HOW EQUIPMENT JUST SEEMS TO FIX ITSELF SOMETIMES.

Ed Wiens © 1999

SINCE YOU'RE ALL "NEWBIES", LET ME EXPLAIN A FEW BASICS ...

COMPUT

THE KEYBOARD IS IN STANDARD "QWERTY" FOR ASCII. THE COMPUTER COMES WITH A SCSI PORT AND THE MONITOR DISPLAYS IN THE USUAL WYSIWYG.

01.27.00

...NOOBEE, KWERTEE, ASKEEE, SKUZZEE, WIZZEE-WIGGEEE...

OH GREAT! NOW EVEN BABIES UNDERSTAND THIS STUFF BEFORE I DO!!

MAYBE HE CAN TRANSLATE FOR US?

Ed Wiens © 2000

Ed Wiens © 1997 12.25.97

Ed Wiens © 1997 06.19.97

I HAD A HECK OF A TIME GETTING THIS PRINTER RIBBON OUT OF YOUR PRINTER. WHERE DO YOU KEEP YOUR SPARES?

?!!

YOU DIDN'T OPEN THE PRINTER! YOU OPENED THE **CPU**!!

SO, WHAT'S THIS THING THEN?

I BELIEVE THE HUMAN EQUIVALENT WOULD BE A **SPINAL COLUMN**!

Ed Wiens © 1997 06.05.97

FOOSH!

WHRRRRRR...

BLINK!

FOOSH!

WHRRRRRRR...

BLINK! HOW MANY POWER FAILURES CAN THERE **BE** IN ONE DAY?!

NO. NO... NOW I'M SURE. **THIS** IS THE BREAKER FOR THE OUTSIDE OUTLETS!

Ed Wiens © 1997 04.24.97

CHAPTER THREE

GLitcH!
Unplugged

MICRO-GLITCH
PRINCIPLE #78
...

ALWAYS
CAREFULLY
CHECK OUT
YOUR
PERIPHERAL
CHAIN.

LET'S SEE... COMPUTER, EXTERNAL REMOVEABLE HARDDRIVE, CD-ROM WRITER, SCANNER, MODEM, MIX-MASTER. I DON'T SEE WHERE THE PROBLEM IS.

Ed Wiens © 2000 02.10.00

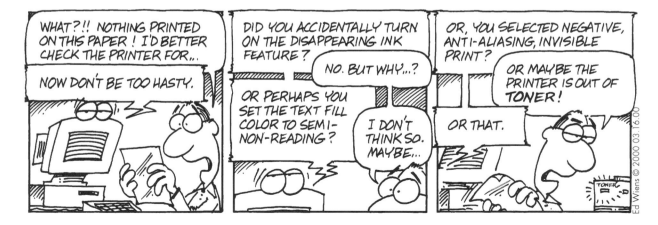

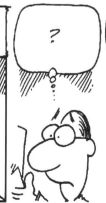

Ed Wiens © 1997 03.05.98

Ed Wiens © 1998 10.22.98

CHAPTER FOUR

GLitcH!

Sales & Disservice

WE'LL CALL YOU WHEN IT'S READY. THEN YOU WON'T HAVE TO BE WHACKING IT ON THE SIDE OR WIGGLING WIRES TO GET IT TO WORK ANY MORE, HA, HA, HA, HA...!

COMPUTER SERVICE

I DON'T GET IT! THE ONLY THING THAT WORKS IS WHACKING IT ON THE SIDE OR WIGGLING ITS WIRES!

BLEEP

Ed Wiens © 1999 08.19.99

IF YOU WANT TO GO "CADILLAC," THIS LITTLE NUMBER CAN'T BE BEAT! IT COMES WITH ALL THE OPTIONS.

OR TRY THIS: A "ROLLS-ROYCE" OF COMPUTERS WITH THE SPEED OF A "FERRARI!"

SEEING AS YOU SPEAK MAINLY IN AUTOMOTIVE TERMS, HOW WOULD YOU RATE MY GLITCH-1000? MERCEDES? CORVETTE?

...SOMEWHERE BETWEEN AN **EDSEL** AND A **PINTO** WITH TWO FLAT TIRES.

Ed Wiens © 1997 02.13.97

GETTING OUT A JAMMED DISK? WELL, THIS MODEL HAS A LITTLE BUTTON THAT JETTISONS THE DISK BACK OUT.

KERCHUNK

..., AND THIS MODEL REQUIRES YOU STICK A STRAIGHTENED PAPER CLIP INTO THIS LITTLE HOLE TO DISLODGE IT.

INGENIOUS. BUT WHAT ABOUT THE GLITCH-1000 MODEL?

THE GLITCH-1000? I'VE NEVER REALLY HEARD OF GETTING DISKS BACK **OUT** AGAIN. I USUALLY JUST LET IT **KEEP** THEM!

Ed Wiens © 1999 02.18.99

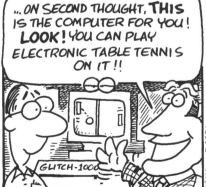

(HUFF, PUFF) WHEW! MADE IT! I'D LIKE TO HAVE SOME COLOR LASER PRINTS MADE... FILES ARE ON THE HARD DISK.

INSTEAD OF LUGGING YOUR COMPUTER ALL THE WAY HERE, WHY DIDN'T YOU SIMPLY COPY YOUR FILES ONTO A FLOPPY DISK?

WOULD YOU BELIEVE I'M DOING HIGHLY CLASSIFIED RESEARCH ON THE EFFECTS OF FRESH AIR ON DIGITAL DATA?

NEXT, CAN WE GO TO THE ZOO?

Ed Wiens © 1999 08.12.99

[CLICK] "HELLO, YOU HAVE REACHED MICRO-GLITCH. FOR SERVICE IN ENGLISH PRESS "ONE." FOR SERVICE IN BINARY PRESS "ONE-ZERO, ONE-ONE, ZERO-ZERO, ONE-ONE-ONE."

"TO OBTAIN ASSISTANCE WITH DISTINGUISHING BETWEEN HARDWARE AND PACKING FOAM, PRESS "*."

"IF YOU REQUIRE A SALES-PERSON, PRESS "NINE." IF YOU WANT TO GET RID OF A SALES PERSON, PRESS "NINE-ONE-ONE."

"AND FOR TECHNICAL SERVICE PRESS YOUR NOSE INTO THE MANUAL THAT CAME WITH THE PRODUCT BEFORE BUGGING US." [CLICK!]

AND THEY SAY CUSTOMER SERVICE IS DEAD IN THE DIGITAL AGE.

Ed Wiens © 1998 12.10.98

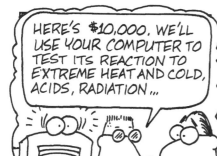

NOPE, I THINK THAT'S ONE COMPUTER CRASH THAT WE **CAN'T** RECOVER.

Ed Wiens © 1997 08.27.98

IT SEEMS THAT SOMEONE OR **SOMETHING** GAVE ME SOME INCORRECT ADVICE ABOUT HARD DRIVES!

WHAT DO YOU MEAN?

WHEN I WALKED INTO THE COMPUTER STORE AND **SPECIFICALLY** ASKED FOR A HARD DRIVE THAT CAN STORE A "MEGGA-GIGGA-GARGANTU-BLOATO-BYTE," THE SALESMEN WERE ON THE FLOOR LAUGHING SO HARD THAT THEY WERE **NO** HELP!

OH, I'M SORRY, IS THAT WHAT I SAID TO BUY? I MEANT A DRIVE THAT CAN STORE A "GIVVA-DOGGA-BYTE." YOU'D BETTER GO BACK.

HOW DO YOU SPELL THAT?

Ed Wiens © 1999 03.18.99

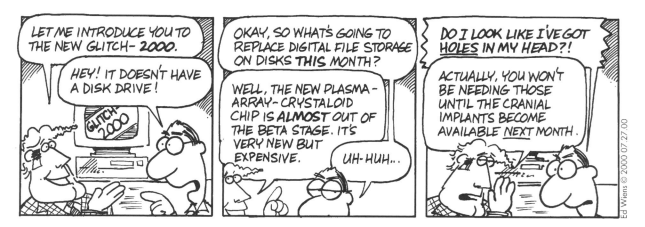

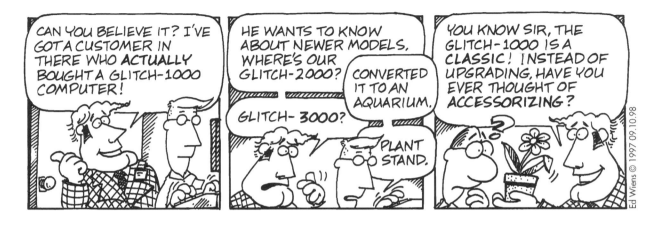

DO YOU SEE ANY FOOTPRINTS ON MY FOREHEAD?

NO, WHY?

BECAUSE COMPUTER SALESMEN SEEM TO TAKE PERVERSE PLEASURE IN GOING OVER MY HEAD WITH TECHNICAL LINGO! SOMEHOW I GOT RIDICULED FOR NOT UNDERSTANDING THE LATEST TECHNOLOGY; GOT SIGNED UP FOR A COMPUTER COURSE; HAD TO BUY A NEW DVD DRIVE; AND NOW I HAVE TO BRING YOU IN FOR AN UPGRADE!

WHAT'S WRONG WITH THAT?

I WENT IN TO BUY A **MOUSE PAD**!

Ed Wiens © 2000 10.26.00

SORRY. NO REFUNDS.

I DON'T **WANT A REFUND. DON'T YOU REMEMBER ME? I JUST BOUGHT THIS COMPUTER FROM YOU 30 SECONDS AGO!**

NO TRADE-INS THEN.

I JUST CAME BACK IN BECAUSE I FORGOT MY RECEIPT.

YOU SEE THAT DOOR? ONCE YOU STEP OUTSIDE, YOUR COMPUTER DROPS IN VALUE BY 75%.

03.02.00

BESIDES, THE LAST GLITCH-1000s WE TOOK BACK ALL LEAKED.

"LEAKED?" SO **THAT'S** WHY ALL YOUR AQUARIUMS HAVE DISK DRIVES!

Ed Wiens © 2000

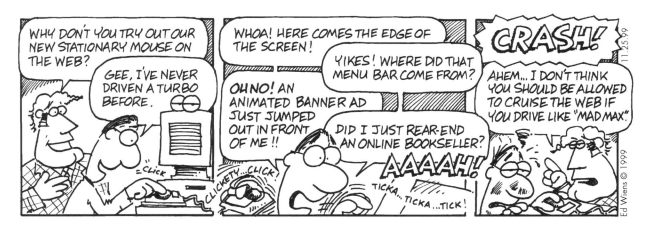

CHAPTER FIVE
The GLitcH! Biz

I USED TO THINK THAT WORKING ON A COMPUTER WOULD LET ME GET THINGS DONE TWICE AS FAST.

WHICH WOULD GIVE ME HALF OF MY WORK TIME FOR LEISURE!

ONLY NOW THEY EXPECT ME TO DO TWICE THE WORK LOAD!

SINCE MY COMPUTER BREAKS DOWN EVERY OTHER DAY, I'M TRYING TO DO **400%** OF MY WORK IN A **QUARTER** OF THE TIME...

LEAVING ME HALF NUTS!

Ed Wiens © 1999

WELCOME TO THE MICRO-GLITCH CUSTOMER SUPPORT HELP HOTLINE. ALL OPERATORS ARE CURRENTLY BUSY CHECKING THEIR STOCK OPTIONS...

ALSO NOTE THAT ALL SYSTEM PROGRAMMERS WILL BE UNAVAILABLE FROM 1 TO 2 PM AS THAT IS THEIR NAP TIME...

BROADCAST MESSAGE FROM THE CEO'S MOMMY: "DON'T BE LOOKING FOR ANY MORE UPGRADES UNTIL A CERTAIN NAUGHTY CEO BEGINS EATING ALL HIS VEGETABLES!"

Ed Wiens © 2000

03.30.00

I HEAR THAT "BANANA" COMPUTER CORPORATION IS IN TROUBLE AGAIN AND MIGHT MERGE WITH MICRO-GLITCH.

THEY SAY THEY MAKE PRETTY GOOD COMPUTERS BUT I DON'T GET WHY THEY CHOSE THAT NAME.

BANANA INC

I MEAN, WHAT DOES A COMPUTER HAVE IN COMMON WITH A FRUIT ANYWAY?

SIMILAR SHELF LIFE?

8.28.97

Ed Wiens © 1997

CHAPTER SIX
The World-Wide-
Glitch!

I WAS JUST READING ABOUT THE RIFT IN SOCIETY BECAUSE OF THE INTERNET: THE INTERNET USERS AND THE GREAT "UNPLUGGED."

WELL, I THINK THE GOVERNMENT SHOULD REGULATE AND FAIRLY ADMINISTRATE EVERYTHING ABOUT THE INTERNET.

CONGRATULATIONS. YOU'VE JUST CREATED A NEW CATEGORY. FIRST THERE WAS THE "PLUGGED-IN," THEN THE "UN-PLUGGED," AND NOW THE "PLUGGED-UP."

Ed Wiens © 1999 09.02.99

GLITCH'S 1st BOOK OF COMPUTER COMICS

HEY! LOOK AT THIS! OUR NEIGHBOURHOOD BUTCHER HAS HIS OWN WEB SITE! I HAD NO IDEA HE WAS SO "WEB-SAVVY."

IT SAYS, "DROP IN FOR THE BEST CYBER-SPICY, DIGITAL-LINK-SAUSAGES, LIVER-WEB-WURST AND FRESHLY GROUND 'RAM' BURGER."

I THINK I'M GOING TO BE "CYBER-SICK."

SPECIAL THIS WEEK ON VIRTUAL VEAL!

Ed Wiens © 1999 01.07.99

LET ME GET THIS STRAIGHT. THE INFORMATION I NEED ON CONNECTING TO THE WEB IS ONLY AVAILABLE ON THE COMPUTER COMPANY'S WEBSITE?

Ed Wiens © 1999 07.22.99

SO? WHAT PART OF THAT DON'T YOU UNDERSTAND?

IT MEANS I HAVE TO FIRST **BE** ON THE WEB IN ORDER TO FIND OUT HOW TO **GET** ON THE WEB!! IT'S A **CATCH-22!**

I'M SORRY, IF YOU WANT TO SPEW MEANINGLESS ALPHA-NUMERIC CHARACTERS AT ME, YOU'LL NEED TO GET ME AN UPGRADE.

LET ME GUESS: YOU CAN ONLY UPGRADE **NEW** COMPUTERS, RIGHT?

SO, HAVE YOU HEARD ABOUT THIS NEW WIRELESS INTERNET?

LET ME GET THIS STRAIGHT...

YOU COULD NOW TAKE A COMPUTER WITH YOU ANYWHERE IN THIS HOUSE, EVEN A ROOM WITHOUT A TELEPHONE OUTLET —LIKE THE BATHROOM— AND STILL BE ABLE TO SIT DOWN AND GET CONNECTED TO THE INTERNET?

THAT'S RIGHT. WHAT DO YOU THINK?

GLAD I'M NOT A LAPTOP.

IT'S INTERESTING THAT ALL THE POLITICAL PARTIES IN THIS LAST ELECTION HAD THEIR OWN WEB SITES.

...NEARLY WORE OUT MY "DOUBLE-SPEAK" FILTER...

NOT ONLY COULD YOU VIEW THEIR WEB PAGES IN FULL GRAPHICS OR "TEXT-ONLY" BUT ALSO IN "TRUTH-ENHANCED" MODE...!

...OR MY FAVORITE BROWSER MODE, "LUCID DREAMING IN FAIRY TALE TECHNICOLOR."

... INVOLVES SEEING THE WORLD THROUGH A ROSE-COLORED MONITOR!

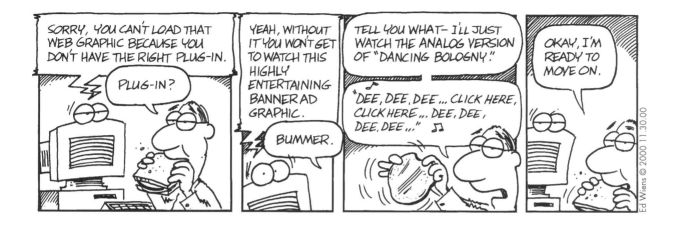

I NOTICE A TREND.

A FRIEND OR RELATIVE BUYS A COMPUTER. GETS INTERNET. SUDDENLY, ALL I GET IS EMAIL CONSISTING OF CARTOONS AND RECIPES ALONG WITH A STEADY BABBLING STREAM ABOUT WHETHER THEY GOT THE ADDRESS OR ATTACHMENTS RIGHT. BUT THEY DON'T WRITE ANYTHING THAT MIGHT ACTUALLY BE INTERESTING!!

07.13.00

IT'S KIND OF LIKE GETTING REGULAR MAIL WITH NOTHING BUT NEWSPAPER CLIPPINGS ALONG WITH MUTTERINGS ABOUT THE INK IN THEIR PEN OR WHETHER THE PAPER WILL HOLD OUT THROUGH THE MAIL! WHAT ABOUT "HOW'S THE FAMILY?" THE JOB? THE WEATHER?!!

BEFORE I TELL YOU THE PRINTER IS JAMMED LET ME JUST SAY THAT IN TODAY'S WEATHER EXPECT A 50% CHANCE OF RAIN OR SUNSHINE...

OH, SHUT UP!

Ed Wiens © 2000

THIS COMPUTER MANUAL DOESN'T INSPIRE A LOT OF CONFIDENCE. LOOK HERE...

"CHAPTER ONE: INTERNET ACCESS WITH THE PUSH OF ONE BUTTON."

WHAT'S WRONG WITH THAT?

CHAPTERS 2-38 ARE ON WHAT TO DO WHEN THAT BUTTON DOESN'T WORK!

Ed Wiens © 2000 09.21.00

THIS ONLINE AUCTION STUFF IS BIZARRE. LOOK AT THIS — HALF-USED DEODORANTS OWNED BY CELEBRITIES. HOO BOY, THE STUFF YOU FIND!

WHY DON'T YOU CHECK THE HALF-**BRAIN** SECTION. MAYBE YOU CAN FIND A REPLACEMENT FOR YOUR MISSING HALF!

"UP FOR BID: ONE GLITCH-1000 COMPUTER. OPENING BID: ONE TWIST-TIE."

Ed Wiens © 2000 06.29.00

AH, IT'S GOOD TO BE HOME KNOWING THAT MY COMPUTER, LIKE A FAITHFUL DOG, IS WAITING TO FETCH THE LATEST NEWS FROM THE WEB FOR ME AND AMUSE AND ENTERTAIN ME WITH A GAME OR TWO.

BEEP

AAAAAAH! BZZZZT! THERE GOES SYSTEM CRASH #56!! DO YOU SMELL SMOKE? I THINK I'M ON FIRE!!

I SHOULD'VE BOUGHT A CAT.

WHERE'S THAT VIRUS PROTECTION SOFTWARE I TOLD YOU TO BUY? AND DID YOU BACK UP YOUR FILES? NO! IF I TOLD YOU ONCE I TOLD YOU A THOUSAND TIME...!

Ed Wiens © 1999 12.02.99

CHAPTER SEVEN
Backup on Floppy
GLitcH!

PRINT MY FILE.

NO.

START MY PROGRAM.

NO.

SAVE MY DOCUMENT.

NO.

TICKA... TICKA... TICKA... TICK...

I DON'T GET IT!! I JUST GAVE YOU A MEMORY AND SPEED UPGRADE, AND YOU **STILL** WON'T DO WHAT I WANT!!

IF YOU HAD BEEN PAYING **CAREFUL** ATTENTION, YOU WOULD HAVE NOTICED THAT I CAN NOW REJECT YOUR REQUEST **TWICE** AS FAST!

Ed Wiens © 1999

THE "GLITCH-CODE" PROGRAMMERS GUIDE TO...

THE "HELP" UTILITY HIERARCHY CHART

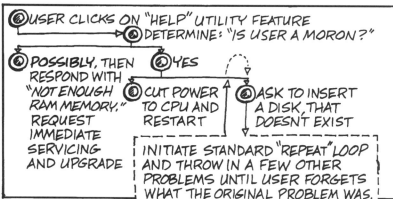

USER CLICKS ON "HELP" UTILITY FEATURE

DETERMINE: "IS USER A MORON?"

POSSIBLY, THEN RESPOND WITH "NOT ENOUGH RAM MEMORY." REQUEST IMMEDIATE SERVICING AND UPGRADE

YES

CUT POWER TO CPU AND RESTART

ASK TO INSERT A DISK, THAT DOESN'T EXIST

INITIATE STANDARD "REPEAT" LOOP AND THROW IN A FEW OTHER PROBLEMS UNTIL USER FORGETS WHAT THE ORIGINAL PROBLEM WAS.

Ed Wiens © 1998 08.13.98

"AT THIS JUNCTURE YOU WILL BE MOST LIKING TO IMPLICATE NICELY CABLES "X" AND 4..."

"... BINARY PROTOCOLS ARE ASSEMBLED IN RIGOROUS CIRCUMSPECT BY HOMELY FASHION..."

I'M NOT SURE IF THIS IS SIMPLY A POOR ENGLISH TRANSLATION OR WHETHER IT IS ACCURATELY WRITTEN IN "TECHNO-SPEAK!"

Ed Wiens © 1996 08.15.96

WHAT ARE YOU READING?

"THE MORON'S GUIDE TO WORD-PROCESSING: SOFTWARE AND YOU — FRIENDS FOR LIFE."

OF COURSE, THIS "FRIEND" WILL NEED TO BE PAID OFF CONTINUOUSLY IN ORDER TO GET UPDATED VERSIONS OF THIS HERE "FRIEND." EVENTUALLY IT WILL NEED TO BE REPLACED BY A NEWER, BIGGER "FRIEND" WHO WILL TAKE LONGER TO GET TO KNOW AND WHO WILL THEN JUST UP AND QUIT ON YOU WHENEVER IT WANTS ...!

YOU KNOW... YOU'RE A BITTER, BITTER MAN. NO WONDER YOU'VE ONLY GOT SOFTWARE FOR FRIENDS.

Ed Wiens © 2001 01.18.01

WELCOME TO OUR MANDATORY COMPUTER PROGRAM TRAINING SESSION SEMINAR 101, BEGINNER LEVEL.

STEP ONE: BEGIN BY READING ALL SIX VOLUMES OF THE SOFTWARE MANUALS. THEN... FOLLOW THOSE PROCEDURES EXACTLY.

?   ?

Ed Wiens © 1999 06.10.99

...UNLESS, OF COURSE, YOU ENCOUNTER THE SPECIAL CIRCUMSTANCES AS LISTED IN APPENDICES "A" THROUGH "P."

A USER'S GUIDE TO THE GLITCH-1000 COMPUTER

PRINCIPLE # 1 THE URGENCY IN YOUR VOICE AND ACTIONS DETERMINES THE PROBABILITY OF A COMPUTER SHUT-DOWN.

START UP!! PLEASE, PLEASE PLEASE...

SLIGHT ANXIETY. GOOD. THAT'S ABOUT AN 8.5...

WORK, YOU DARN PROGRAM! WORK, WORK, WORK!

STRESS LEVEL RISING UP TO 9.5.

CAREFUL, CAREFUL NOW... PRINT, PRINT, PRINT, PRINT!

WE HAVE A WINNER! SHUT-DOWN ENGAGED!

BING!

Ed Wiens © 1999

OKAY, TO ENTER DATA INTO YOUR SPREAD-SHEET, FIRST YOU CLICK ON A CELL...

CELL?

WHY, THERE'S NOTHING BUT TINY, EMPTY CELLS AS FAR AS I CAN SCROLL UP, DOWN, LEFT OR RIGHT...

THERE'S MILLIONS OF THEM!

THE WALLS ARE CLOSING IN ON ME! I CAN'T... BREATHE!

CALM DOWN! YOU'RE JUST ENTERING SOME NUMBERS!

...AND NEXT YOU'LL BE ENTERING SOME FORMULAS.

DID I MENTION I FAILED CHEMISTRY?

09.18.97

Ed Wiens © 1997

I CAN'T BELIEVE THIS! FIRST, THEY WANT ME TO UPGRADE MY PROGRAM TO VERSION 2.0...

AND WHEN I DON'T, ONE MONTH LATER THEY SEND ME THE SAME ORDER FORM, ONLY NOW THEY'RE GIVING AWAY SOME FREE CHEAPO CLIP-ART AND UTILITIES. WHAT KIND OF MORON DO THEY THINK I AM?

IT COMES WITH A FREE MICRO-GLITCH KEYCHAIN.

SOLD!

Ed Wiens © 1999 02.11.99

IS THIS THE RIGHT TRAINING ROOM FOR CORPORATE SEMINAR 303: "MANDATORY SOFTWARE INSTRUCTION AND WHY I'LL LIKE IT"?

UH...

ROOM B

Ed Wiens © 1999 08.26.99

SORRY. THIS IS THE "UNTRAINED INSTRUCTOR'S GUIDE TO BACK-UP PROCEDURES."

...WRITE OUT A COPY IN PENCIL, PLACE IN A COFFEE CAN AND BURY IT IN YOUR BACK YARD.

MAYBE CHECK DOWN THE HALL. I HEAR "SOFTWARE WE'RE ALL HYPED ABOUT, BUT WHICH DOESN'T EXIST YET" IS JUST LETTING OUT.

...IN CLOSING, THE FUTURE MIGHT BE HERE... TOMORROW!

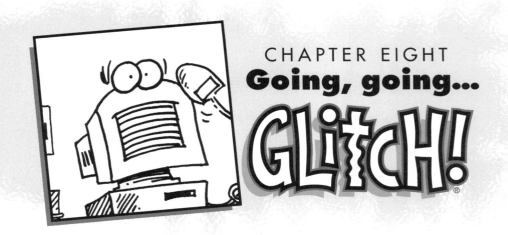

CHAPTER EIGHT

Going, going...
GLitcH!

I JUST READ THAT THE BOOK VALUE ON A SYSTEM EXACTLY LIKE YOU IS ONLY HALF OF WHAT I PAID SIX MONTHS AGO!

LET'S REVIEW THAT.

SEEING AS MY NET WORTH IS DOWN 50%, THAT MEANS YOU PAID TWICE THE REPLACEMENT COST, REQUIRING GREATER INVESTMENT... ...CARRY THE TWO...!

THE WAY I SEE IT YOU SHOULD VALUE ME **TWICE** AS MUCH BECAUSE TO YOU I'M WORTH **200%** CURRENT VALUE!!

07.30.98

Ed Wiens © 1998

CHAPTER NINE
Me and my
GLitcH!

HEY! WHERE DID MY CURSOR GO?!!

ABOUT 23 MILLION KILOMETRES TO THE LEFT.

WHAT?!

YOU'VE GOT THE MOUSE VELOCITY SET TO "LIGHTSPEED." HERE, TRY THE ONE OTHER OPTION: "SNAIL SPEED."

AAGH! ✪☆#@!? ?✳%!!!☆!

NOW YOU KNOW WHY THEY CALL THEM "CURSORS."

Ed Wiens © 2000 03.09.00

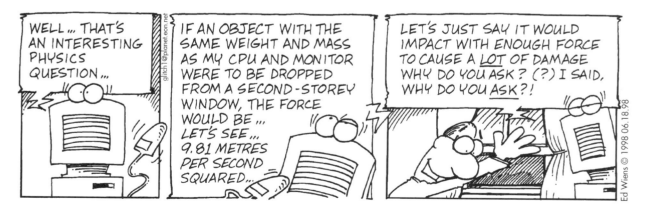

Ed Wiens © 1997 02.27.97

Ed Wiens © 1997 11.20.97

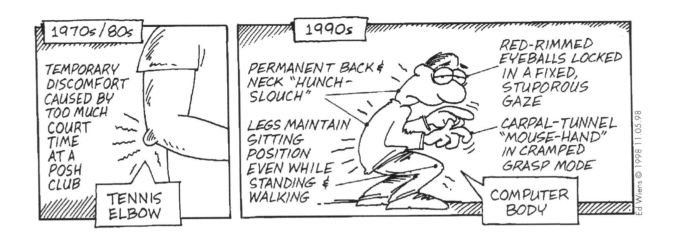

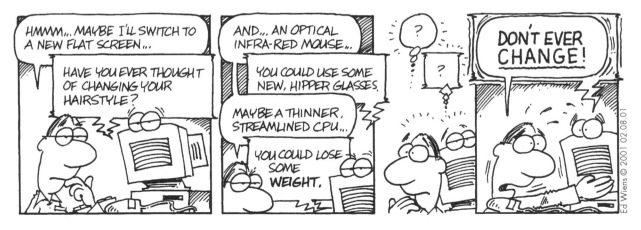

The Comic Strip

GLitcH! is a self-syndicated entertainment feature that has enjoyed success on the web, appearing on four different websites for major Canadian telecommunications companies. The comic strip also consistently appears in over a million pieces of print per month in major news and tabloid publications across Canada.

GLitcH! has been enjoyed by a wide audience ranging from children to seniors and from absolute beginners on the computer to expert programmers. E-mail has been received from readers from across North America, many with the same comment:

"My computer is just like that!"

Take a look at GLitcH! on the web at:

www.glitch.ca

The Cartoonist

Ed Wiens writes and draws the computer-based comic strip, "GLitcH!" which has been self-syndicated to a national audience in Canada for newspapers, computer trade magazines, newsletters, educational publications, postcards and for the web since 1996.

Ed grew up in British Columbia's Okanagan Valley and later moved to Edmonton, Alberta to study Visual Communications at the University of Alberta. After University, he worked first as a graphic designer mainly for the oil industry and then later for the Government of Alberta where, as part of a capital development team, became an award-winning designer for graphics and exhibition design for work on many of the major museums, interpretive centres and historic sites in the province.

In addition to GLitcH!, Ed continues to develop entertainment features as well as produce graphics for history and heritage projects.

Ed Wiens lives in Edmonton, Alberta with his wife and two children.